Mont Saint-Michel

Text **Lucien Bély**   Photography **Hervé Champollion**

Translation **id2m**

Editions OUEST-FRANCE

The history of Mont Saint-Michel

Back cover

FRÉMIET'S STATUE OF SAINT MICHAEL
after its restoration in 1987.
Photo: Brother François Lancelot, Mont-Saint-Michel Abbey.

THE CLOISTERS.

Visiting Mont Saint-Michel

The history of Mont Saint-Michel

Between rocks and sea

Try to imagine Mont Saint-Michel before anything was built on it. This sheer-sided granite rock, rising eighty metres out of the sea, has resisted erosion from wind and water for thousands of years. This mound, along with a handful of others, dominates the surrounding low-lying region.

The sea engulfed the land around the Mont, probably as long ago as the Bronze Age, and prehistoric fishing grounds prove that the bay has long had plentiful fish. However, historians used to think that a forest, called the forest of Scissy, once surrounded the area. This was reputed to have disappeared when the sea gradually engulfed it. The discovery of remains of trees buried in the sands seemed to confirm this notion. According to legend, a tidal wave definitively transformed the landscape sometime at

A BIRD'S-EYE VIEW OF THE MONT FROM THE EAST.
The rock stands in the middle of the strands covered in grey silt, criss-crossed by rivers and sea currents. The causeway that provides access to the Mont has undoubtedly inhibited the free flow of water, thus transforming the landscape of the bay.
Photo: Thierry Seni.

THE FAMOUS MOUTONS PRÉS-SALÉS.
The Mont rises out of the sands, the village at the foot of the rock and the monastery at the top.

the start of the 8th century, at the exact moment when Bishop Aubert dedicated the Mont to Saint Michael, turning it into an island like the neighbouring mound of Tombelaine. Nowadays, it is believed that tides continually swept the bay but that these drew back occasionally, allowing copses to form.

In any event, tidal reaches in the Bay of Mont Saint-Michel, calculated by measuring the difference between low and high tide at the same location, often exceed twelve meters, one of the largest in the world. The surrounding strands are almost completely flat and the sea comes in over a

dozen miles in the space of a few hours, as fast as a horse at full gallop. This can be very dangerous for unwary shrimp fishermen and walkers. At times, the sea travels under the sand, creating pockets of treacherous quicksand.

Three rivers - the Sée, the Sélune and the Couesnon - flow out onto the strand. The latter marks the boundary between Brittany and Normandy for, as the old saying goes: "The Couesnon's act of folly left the Mont in Normandy." The grey silt, known locally as *tangue*, gives the landscape its delicate colouring. Salt-resistant plants such as marsh samphire and sea fennel colonised silted-up areas of the shore that are no longer covered by high tide. Grass soon took over and the sheep that graze there are known locally as *prés-salés* because of the salty flavour of their meat.

At the meeting point of sand, sea and sky, a citadel-like abbey was built standing almost seventy metres tall at its highest point, the church spire.

The hermits

A new religion – Christianity – appeared during the declining years of the Roman empire. Men who believed in one, unique God and his son Jesus criss-crossed Europe, driving out the gods of Rome and the old gods of the woods and lakes alike. To escape earthly pleasures, austere Christians, known as hermits, chose to live in complete poverty deep in forests or on deserted islands. The place we now call Mont Saint-Michel was originally known as Mont Tombe, meaning both a tomb and a hill. It may have been an ancient place of worship but there is no proof of this. In any case, this mound must have attracted the hermits, as Christians settled very quickly around the bay and near Dol-de-Bretagne. A legend tells how fishermen provided food to the solitary hermits on the Mont, carried by a donkey guided by God.

At the same time, in the early Middle Ages, the Christian church was becoming organised, with bishops placed in the main towns charged with tending the souls of the populace. It also singled out remarkable men and women, calling them "saints" and offering them to the faithful as objects of worship after their death. The Archangel Saint Michael was worshipped from the Orient to Gaul.

THE SALISBURY BREVIARY tells how the sanctuary was born. The Archangel watches over the pilgrim who has come to see Bishop Aubert, seen below striking the rock with his crosier to create a spring. At the bottom of the page is a portrayal of the first mass and the ramparts as they were in the 15th century.

Paris, BNF (National Library of France), latin ms 17294.

Aubert dedicates the rock to Saint Michel

The Archangel Saint Michael often appeared in Italy, at Monte Gargano, a rocky peninsula on the Adriatic Sea and in Rome, at the Moles Hadriani, near the castle that still bears his name (Castel di Sant Angelo).

Legend has it that one night during the year 708, Aubert, Bishop of the nearby town of Avranches, was visited by Saint Michael in a dream and was ordered to turn the Mont into a shrine to him. Aubert, thinking he had imagined it, did nothing. The archangel grew impatient with him and, when he appeared for the third time, he poked a hole in the disbeliever's skull. He performed many miracles to convince the bishop and Christians. A stolen bull was found at the top of the Mont, as Saint Michael had predicted. According to one story, Aubert's oratory was built on the area of land trampled by the bull. According to another, the ora-

tory was built on the area left dry by the morning dew.

Aubert fulfilled the archangel's wishes and sent messengers to Monte Gargano in Italy. They brought back sacred relics, including a piece of the red cloak worn by the archangel during one of his apparitions and a fragment of the altar where he had placed his foot.

Upon their return, Aubert built the sanctuary. Divine intervention facilitated the men's work. An old man from the locality, called by God, managed to move a large rock. According to another version, it was a child that touched the rock with his foot, sending it tumbling into the abyss. Although there was no drinking water on the mount, a spring, the fountain of Saint-Aubert, was miraculously discovered. The consecration of the Mont, for which there is no historic documentation apart from a much later account, the *Revelatio*, thus gave rise to marvellous legends that enchanted Christians and on which the first historians later relied.

As time went by, the rock became known as Mont Saint-Michel and Aubert sent some men to live there and pray to God and his archangel.

Above

THE CHAPEL OF SAINT-AUBERT,
on the seashore, bears the name
of the bishop of Avranches who founded the sanctuary.

Saint Michael
According to the Bible, the archangels Michael, Raphael and Gabriel - soldiers and messengers of God - rank higher than angels. When Satan, the fallen angel, compared himself to God, another angel stood before him and shouted "Mi-ka-ël" (Michael), i.e. who is like God? God entrusted his armies to Michael the "Prince of the Angels". This tradition was carried over to Christianity and the archangel became Saint Michael. In the *Book of Revelation* by Saint John, a seven-headed dragon, with a tail so long it swept the stars, threatened the Virgin and newborn Christ child. Michael and his angels fought this evil serpent of Satan and slew him. Michael is portrayed first with huge wings, wearing a long white tunic, and then brandishing a flaming spear or sword. He leads the souls and often incarnates the forces of earth, and is associated with natural phenomena that fire the imagination, such as lightning, light and comets, and with amazing geological phenomena such as steep mountains and rocks pounded by the sea, such as Mont Saint-Michel.

Right page
SAINT AUBERT, BISHOP OF AVRANCHES,
had a vision of Saint Michael who ordered him to turn the rock into a shrine dedicated to him. The saint poked a hole in Aubert's forehead to convince him that it wasn't just a dream. Musicians can be seen playing in the windows of the handsome construction where the scene took place. The origin of the Mont Saint-Michel closely resembles that of the sanctuary near Monte Gargano, on the Adriatic coast.
Cartulaire du Mont Saint-Michel, c. 1150, Avranches, ms 210, folio 4 verso.

Founding the abbey

The peace and prosperity brought about by Charlemagne did not last long. Norsemen, or Normans, regularly pillaged the coastline. They finally settled and the King of the Franks recognised one of their chiefs, Rollo the Rover, as Duke of Normandy. In exchange, the formidable warrior became a Christian, along with all his soldiers, and from then on protected all those in the service of God.

Rollo and his descendants rebuilt important sanctuaries destroyed by the Normans. However, the newly converted were very imperious. Duke Richard reproached the priests living on the Mont for their immoral and impious behaviour. He threw them out and replaced them in 966 with submissive and humble monks from Flanders, guided by a man of noble family called Maynard. The eleven monks adopted the rule of Saint Benedict, which required them to live according to the principles of poverty, chastity and obedience and the abbey became a Benedictine abbey.

The father of the community, the abbot, administered the monastery's possessions, encouraged the cult of Saint Michael and received visitors. Theoretically, the monks themselves elected their superior, but in practice, the Duke of Normandy, as protector of the abbey, imposed his own candidate. This led to quite a number of quarrels and conflicts. However, some abbots, through their faith, authority and generosity, won the admiration of all, for example, Bernard du Bec in the 12th century.

The Benedictines

A MONK PRAYING
Histoire du Mont Saint-Michel,
Avranches, ms 213, folio 229.

Saint Benedict founded a monastery at Monte Cassino in the 6th century where he drew up a Rule to organise the life of those who wished to devote themselves to prayer and the glorification of God. He introduced eastern monastic practices into the Western world. The Rule of Saint Benedict was applied to all of the monks' activity. It was strict as regards spirituality but more flexible when it came to dealing with material issues, allowing men and women to live communally. In 1958, Saint Benedict was declared "Father of Europe and Patron of the West".

Normandy

Originally pillaging pagans, the Normans settled on the coast of the Channel and converted to Christianity. This led to the establishment of a dominion, the subjugation of the populace by the newcomers and the construction of a strong state. The monks, attracted by the new-found piety of the Norman dukes, flocked to Normandy as missionaries. The Dukes of Normandy were supported by the Benedictine abbots and monks such as those at Mont Saint-Michel. Although the Duke recognised the authority of his weak neighbour, the King of the Franks or of France, the duchy actually remained more or less independent for a long time, especially when it was allied with the kingdom of England. Later, in 1214, victory at the Battle of Bouvines, Normandy became a province of the kingdom of France.

Above
THE ABBEY SEEN FROM THE SOUTH-EAST.
In the foreground, the abbot's house reminds us that the abbot was the father of the community, at the head of a vast ensemble of seigneuries and lands.

Left page
THE MONT SAINT-MICHEL was one of the wonders of France chosen to adorn the manuscript of Très Riches Heures, a book of hours by the Duke of Berry, brother of King Charles V. Apart from the beauty of the composition, dominated by the fight between a feather-clad Michael and the dragon, the accuracy of detail makes this document highly valuable, showing as it does the town with its houses overlooking the strands. Above all, the artist wanted to render the beauty of the grand abbey with its high walls and pointed bell towers.
Musée Condé - Photo: RMN © René-Gabriel Ojéda.

The Romanesque period

The monks' vocation was to pray for themselves, their families and for all men. Most of them were from the nobility or knights' families, the only ones in feudal society allowed to bear arms. Behind the high walls of the monastery in the 'enclosure' they avoided all worldly temptations and violence as far as they could. Their day was divided into eight canonical hours: Matins, at daybreak, Lauds, Prime, Terce, Sext at midday and Nones, Vespers and Compline at nightfall. There were specific prayers for each of these hours, set out in the monks' book of hours. And on top of that masses were held.

When the old buildings were no longer large enough to house the monks and receive pilgrims, who were starting to flock there in large numbers, the abbey expanded, thanks to the protection and wealth of the Duke of Normandy. It took almost one hundred years to complete this Romanesque complex. One of the oldest buildings, Notre-Dame-sous-Terre (Our Lady Underground) was given a vault that characterised the latest building techniques and architectural fancies. The crypt, Notre-Dame-des-Trente-Cierges (Our Lady of the Thirty Candles), was built beneath the church and supports

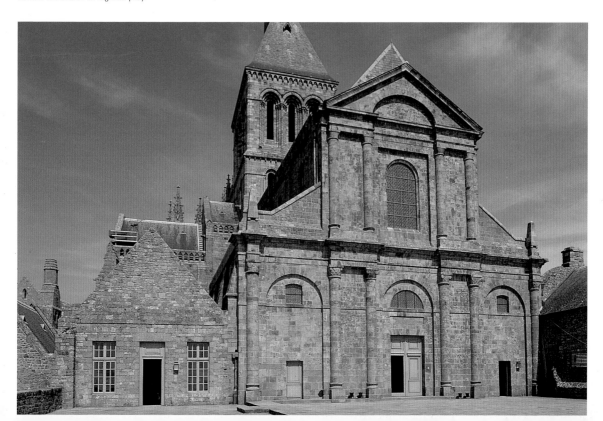

William the Conqueror

The Normans retained a taste for military adventure and sea-faring expeditions. They launched the conquest of England. William, the illegitimate son of Duke Robert, managed to impose his rule in Normandy and within ten months of the death of Edward the Confessor, King of England, he had boats built to travel across the Channel and vanquish his English rival, Harold, at the Battle of Hastings in 1066. William the Conqueror then became King of England. For the next four hundred years, the history of Normandy was inextricably linked with that of England. As the same nobility ruled over both countries, the Norman monks left to assist the King in his new kingdom and head up the English church.

Below

THE BAYEUX TAPESTRY.
This huge tapestry recounts the story of William the Conqueror. Before conquering England, the duke launched an expedition against the Bretons. William and his army came to the Mont, portrayed here as a shrine atop a mound, and then crossed the Couesnon river, where some of the soldiers got stuck in the sand.
By special permission of the town of Bayeux.

THE ROMANESQUE NAVE.
As a historic monument, the sanctuary requires substantial ongoing preservation work, as this postcard from the early 20th century shows.
Henry Decaëns Collection.

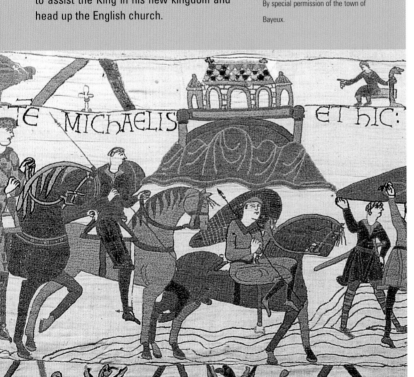

the northern arm of the transept. The semicircular barrel vault of the Chapel of Saint-Martin bears the weight of the southern transept. The monks appreciated the stone vaulting, which improved acoustics for Gregorian chant. The solidity of the huge church, built right at the top of the Mont and completed in 1084, was based on a framework of pillars and arches rather than on a massive pile of stones, demonstrating the advances made in architecture at the time. The arches enabled the galleries and windows to let in more light. As we shall see, the monks' living quarters, known as *conventuels*, occupied three floors in the northern part of the abbey

15th-century pilgrim's badge of **SAINT MICHAEL**.
Musée national du Moyen Âge, Cluny, photo: RMN © Gérard Blot.

THE ARCHANGEL MICHAEL in armour, slaying the dragon and pilgrims arriving at the Mont.
Book of hours by Pierre II, Duke of Brittany, Paris, BNF, latin ms 1159, folio 160 verso.

Famous pilgrims

Very early on, powerful pilgrims came to Mont Saint-Michel to implore the Archangel's protection. Richard II, Duke of Normandy, who married Judith of Brittany here before the nobility of both provinces, endowed the abbey with churches, mills, meadows and forests. The Duke encouraged a religious reform in Normandy under the authority of Guillaume de Volpiano, Abbot of Fécamp.

Thanks to these numerous gifts, the abbey acquired a vast amount of property around the bay. While the individual monks remained poor, the abbey grew richer, making its ceremonies more solemn and its buildings more sumptuous for the greater glory of God. Local peasants, dependant on the abbey, regularly brought part of their harvest over to the island by boat – or by wagon at low tide. In return, they received protection and justice. Many knights also chose to retire to the Mont to prepare for death and find a burial place.

The abbot was obliged to honour the abbey's protectors. When William the Conqueror conquered England, the superior of the Mont sent six ships and four monks to salute the new king. The finest of all the abbots was Robert de Thorigny, who in the 12th century, had been a skilful courtier of King Henry II Plantagenet, who reigned over England and a large part of France. This abbot symbolises the abbey at the peak of its fortunes, enriching the library with rare and precious manuscripts and building vast lodgings for pilgrims in the south-west – the latter collapsed in the early 19th century.

The abbot welcomed a long line of princes to the Mont. King Henry II, of whom he was the adviser, came to visit him, accompanied by Louis VII, King of France, the Archbishop of Rouen, two cardinals who later became popes and five abbots. Their arrival at the abbey was sumptuously celebrated.

The miracles

Because Christianity has an affinity with the world of the supernatural, whenever some strange, fortuitous event occurred on the Mont, it was always attributed to the influence of Saint Michael, demonstrating his presence and power. The monks built up a collection of these miracles, passed down by pilgrims and travellers over the centuries.

One day, a blind woman stood in front of the Mont and, when she turned her face towards it, she recovered her sight. "Qu'il fait beau voir" she said ("How beautiful it is to see") and the village in which she was standing was thereafter called "Beauvoir". Another woman, who was expecting a child, unwisely attempted to cross the strand. She felt the first birth pangs and fell to the sand. The tide was coming in but miraculously the sea spared the young mother. Fishermen later found her and her child safe and sound. A cross, *Croix des Grèves*, marked the spot where this took place. It stood here for several centuries before being swallowed up by the waves.

During the Middle Ages, the bones of saints were believed to have miraculous powers. However, those of Bishop Aubert, who became Saint Aubert, had disappeared. Many years after the abbey was founded, music of divine origin spread throughout the Mont. The monks started searching and found caskets hidden in the dormitory ceiling. A miraculous force caused the locks to spring open and inside were the saint's relics. A parchment proving the authenticity of the bones was also found. Thus for centuries, pilgrims could admire the skull of Aubert, pierced by Saint Michael.

THE ABBEY CHURCH,
with the Romanesque transept
crossing and the Flamboyant chancel,
completed in the early 16th century.

Religious feasts

The people of the Middle Ages enjoyed religious feasts. The architecture of the Mont, with its huge church, mysterious crypts and great staircases, lent itself well to splendid ceremonies.

There were frequent processions through the abbey. On these occasions, the abbot, like a bishop, wore a mitre and carried a crosier. The monks, instead of their usual rough cowls, donned copes, long, sleeveless cloaks or white vestments known as albs. The reliquaries containing the relics and the Gospels were borne aloft among the pilgrims through the candle-lit, incense-clouded monastery. The procession halted at each station of the cross to the sound of fervent prayers.

These ceremonies could turn into veritable theatrical shows. Monks enacted characters from the New Testament so that everyone could understand the sacred texts, similarly to the mystery plays performed in front of cathedrals. In the 12th century, a monk from the Mont, Guillaume de Saint-Pair, wrote a verse sequence recounting the history of the abbey and the miracles that had been wrought there. Unusually for the time, the verses were written in the vernacular and not in Latin, the language of the church. It was called the *Roman du Mont Saint-Michel* and was the work of a monk who had all the qualities of a true minstrel.

Liturgical chant accompanied these ceremonies. The monks were passionate about singing, believing that the human voice enhanced prayer. This plain chant or Gregorian chant, in its

A RELIGIOUS PROCESSION
through the streets of the town on 15 October 1908 for the opening celebrations
of the 12th centenary of the foundation of the Mont by Saint Aubert.
Henry Decaëns Collection.

austerity and simplicity, was a form of worship in itself.

Finally, the reception of a new monk involved a moving ceremony. The young man's head was partly shaved, his tonsure indicating his ecclesiastical vocation. After one year's observation, he took his vows before the entire community. To the accompaniment of songs of praise, the abbot helped him put on a monk's habit and bestowed upon him the kiss of peace. For three days, he prayed in the church. After that, he became one of the monks.

THE CLOISTERS CIRCA 1900
with their glazed tile roof, replaced in 1962 with a schist roof.
Henry Decaëns Collection.

Left page
THE CHURCH CHEVET.
The buttresses, topped with pinnacles and pyramids, decorated with stone flowers and finials, characterise the exuberant flamboyant style, typical of the late Middle Ages and the early 16th century.

Building
the Merveille

In the early 13th century, the great Anglo-Norman kingdom broke up. Philippe Auguste, King of France, took Normandy, which was bloodied by numerous conflicts. Meanwhile, in 1204, an ally of the French king laid siege to the Mont Saint-Michel. The town and abbey were partly destroyed by fire. To obtain pardon and win the monastery over to the French cause, Philippe-Auguste sent a large amount of gold to rebuild the Mont.

The monks, tired of the dark, narrow Romanesque layout, wanted more space and light for their living quarters. The abbots and their architects therefore concentrated on the *conventuels*. During the first half of the 13th century, they built an ensemble of immense rooms spanning three floors, the *Merveille*, a masterpiece of Gothic art.

The architects were extremely daring indeed to attempt to build such a high and vast building on this steep rock. Enormous buttresses were built on the outside to shore up the *Merveille*. As the building grew higher, it had to become lighter to avoid collapse – not an uncommon occurrence. The almonry and cellar on the lower floor have thick walls and strong vaults. On the second floor, the *Salle des Hôtes* [Guest Room] and *Salle des Chevaliers* [Knights' Room] had columns and ribbed vaults to support the refectory and cloister on the third floor.

GROINED VAULTING
gives more height and greater
stability to buildings.

Gothic art

The monks aspired to space, light
and beauty and revolutionary new
techniques in architecture provided these. The barrel vault, much
favoured during the Romanesque
period, was liable to warp and
could not be used in very tall buildings. Soon, two intersecting barrel vaults were used to form a
ceiling for the chapels: this was
groined vaulting. However, this
also tended to warp and, to reinforce the groins, stone-masons
developed the rib vault using pointed arches. The groins were replaced by stone ribs, cut with great
precision and buttressed to carry
the weight. Cunningly balancing
the weight of the arches against
the counterthrust created by exte-
rior buttresses using a skeleton of
columns and arches, the architects were able to erect extremely
high walls, raising roofs to impressive heights and opening out great
bays in the walls without weakening them. To gain stability the
canted arch was often used. This
was the time of the great urban
cathedrals. This was how ogival
art was perfected, an art that was
later despised and called "Gothic"
meaning barbaric.

The life of the monks

From this time on, the monks spent most of their time in the *Merveille*. Poor pilgrims were received in the almonry and noblemen and princes in the *Salle des Hôtes* on the floor above. These two rooms were found near the entrance which, like today, faced east, not north-west as it did during the Romanesque era. The community kept well out of the way on the higher floors of the *Merveille*, near the church.

In the refectory, meals were eaten in silence while one monk read sacred texts from a pulpit. The cloister, suspended in mid-air between sea and sky, was used for strolling, mediation and conversation.

Before the discovery of printing, the only way to preserve and reproduce a text was to copy it by hand. The monks devoted themselves to this work, going to great pains to decorate and adorn manuscripts. This was the art of illumination, where colours and designs were used to illuminate and illustrate letters and pages. The Mont was known as the "city of books", there were many fine works in its library. The monks were interested not only in sacred texts but also in classical works. This meticulous work, and all other work, was carried out in the calefactory or *chauffoir*. This room later became known as the *Salle des Chevaliers* [Knights' Room], and you can just imagine the monks taking refuge there from the cold rising up from the misty sea, fighting it off with fires, tapestries and furs.

ILLUMINATION OF A MANUSCRIPT.

The Benedictine monks set themselves the task of copying and preserving the founding texts of Christian faith. The chief spiritual legacy of the Mont is its collection of manuscripts, now housed in the Scriptorial of Avranches.

Saint Ambroise, Saint Jérôme and Saint Augustine, Œuvres, circa 1060, Avranches, ms. 72, fol. 182.

In any event, the King of France, contrary to the Dukes of Normandy, intervened little in the internal life of the community or the election of abbots – the Mont was now largely independent.

Scriptorial - Musée des manuscrits du Mont Saint-Michel

Place d'Estouteville

50300 Avranches, France

Tel. : 02 33 79 57 00

www.scriptorial.fr

Miquelot pilgrims

In the Middle Ages, everyone was expected to go on a pilgrimage. The richest or bravest went to the Holy Land, Rome or Compostela. Others had to content themselves with a sanctuary that was nearer home. Mont Saint-Michel was, of course, a popular pilgrimage centre for Normans, but it also attracted pilgrims from all over France and western Christendom. Christians went to pray to the Archangel for their sins to be forgiven and for all their hopes to come true. The sick, especially, hoped that a miracle would restore their health, as other people had been cured in the legends of the Mont.

Left

A PILGRIMAGE TO THE MONT, CIRCA 1910.

Henry Decaëns Collection.

Sometimes, God's calling was sudden and inexplicable; one man was said to have set off for the Mont while shoeing a horse, leaving the job unfinished. In 1333, all the parishioners of a village forced their parish priest to follow them to the Mont and say Mass there.

Pilgrims on their way to the Mont were known as *miquelots*. Like all other pilgrims, they could be recognised by their *besace*, a leather pouch carried over the right shoulder and their *bourdon*, a roughly hewn staff.

Scallop shells stitched to their clothing also marked them out as pilgrims.

Pilgrims could expect respect and succour along the way. The roads to Mont Saint-Michel were called "the ways of Paradise" and pilgrims were given shelter for the night in special inns lining these roads or, if sick, they would be cared for in hospices.

Travellers had to run the gauntlet of many dangers along the way, including sickness and fatigue. When they finally beheld the famous Mont, they still had to cross two or three kilo-

Shepherd boys and girls

From the early 14th century onwards, children and teenagers began to make the pilgrimage to Mont Saint-Michel. These children's crusades were the occasion for youthful festivities but also led to disorder, when servants, apprentices and vagabonds joined in the procession. These young pilgrims became known as pastoureaux, or shepherd boys and girls. The children, sometimes as young as 8, came from as far afield as the Rhineland and the south of France. Led by students bearing the effigy of Saint Michael, they gathered behind the standards bearing the coats of arms of their local gentry. These children had sometimes left home against their parents' wishes and were a long way from home. Even though they were helped along the way, fatigue, sickness and death were a constant threat. The political and religious authorities were concerned about these gatherings, which nevertheless continued up to the French Revolution.

metres of tidal flats where they risked quicksand and sudden tidal surges.

A colourful, multilingual medley of the disabled, the sick and pilgrims converged on the Mont, which symbolised their hope of a miracle. Pilgrims also took part in religious feasts. They tried to touch the reliquaries containing the precious relics.

They also made offerings: King Philip the Handsome donated a statue covered in gold, while all the poor had to offer was a stub of wax to light up the chapels.

Travellers ate and slept in the taverns and hostelries of the village nestling at the foot of the abbey. The poorest found refuge in the almonry of the abbey while noblemen were received in the *Salle des Hôtes* or Guest Room. Shops in the village sold pilgrimage badges as souvenirs, particularly brooches of silver or base metal portraying Saint Michael or scallop shells. However pilgrims often made do with a clam or cockle shell gathered on the strand.

The abbey during the Hundred Years' War

Left page

TOUR BOUCLE.

The abbey rising above the town. In the foreground is Tour Boucle, a polygon-shaped bastion, demonstrating how the round tower was replaced by other defence systems in the late Middle Ages.

Above

THE RAMPARTS.

Wars turned the monastery into a citadel that watches over a small walled town. The town walls were themselves fortified with towers, and the sea and strand provided natural protection.

War broke out between France and England in the early 14th century. Coinciding with the plague, which was then spreading throughout Christendom, it devastated the kingdom. The war came to be known as the Hundred Years' War.

After serious French defeats at Poitiers and Crécy, King Charles V began to fight back, aided by his constable, Bertrand Duguesclin. This brave Breton knight, Captain of Mont Saint-Michel, left his wife, Tiphaine Raguenel, under the protection of the archangel when he went off to war. Tiphaine lived in a house at the top of the town, undertaking good works and practising astrology, which fascinated her.

During one of his visits to the abbey,

the mad King Charles VI appointed the Abbot Pierre le Roi, a renowned academic, as his adviser. This man lost no time in fortifying the abbey, protecting the entrance to the monastery with towers and ramparts interspersed with courtyards to create a *châtelet*, or small castle, and barbican. He completed the abbot's house to the south of the Mont where the abbot lived and where administrative and legal affairs were handled.

Normandy fell into the hands of the English in 1415 after the French defeat at the Battle of Agincourt. The Duke of Bedford, brother of the English king, governed the province and won many noble Normans over to his cause. These

included the Abbot of Mont Robert Jolivet, who agreed to advise Bedford and received all of the monastery's goods in recompense.

However, the monks refused to support him in his treachery. A handful of dispossessed knights who had sought refuge with the monks remained faithful to the French cause and to the dauphin Charles, who was to become Charles VII, also known derisively as the King of Bourges.

The Romanesque chancel collapsed around this time and because it was wartime, it was impossible to rebuild it. Like a bad omen, the Couesnon river changed course during a particularly high tide.

Left page

THE MONT SEEN FROM ABOVE.
The fortified character of the abbey is clearly visible here, crowning the rock and ensuring the safety of the monks and their treasures, relics, objects of worship and precious manuscripts.

The fortifications

After the Hundred Years' War, ramparts were built and the abbey was turned into a veritable fortress. The introduction of gun powder gave rise to the development of artillery and, faced with cannons, the round towers and high walls seemed very fragile. The fortifications were built gradually over time, although historians speak of a military "revolution". Tour Boucle is considered one of the earliest and best-preserved testimonies of this evolution. Instead of being round, it was a polygon-shaped, bastion-like construction that heralded the skilful creations of Vauban and others in the 17th century.

Above

THE ABBEY SEEN FROM THE SOUTH.
The ramp, a veritable stone ladder, was used to hoist heavy provisions up the rock towards the Romanesque buildings. Further east is the abbot's house.

The siege of the Mont

The early 15th century was a critical time for Mont Saint-Michel. The English decided to storm this stronghold that dared to stand up to them. Because the citadel, defended by its ramparts and protected by the sea, was impregnable, they decided to starve it into surrender. The siege started in 1424, with numerous troops taking up positions around the bay. A small wooden fort called the *bastille* was built facing the Mont in Ardevon, to keep watch over the shoreline. Finally, a flotilla arrived to complete the blockade from the sea. Some Breton noblemen commanded an expedition from Saint-Malo and skilfully attacked and dispersed the English ships. This naval victory meant that the Mont could again receive provisions by sea. The siege had failed and the citadel had not fallen. For the first time in a long while, the French recovered their confidence.

The miracle was put down to the archangel and devotion to him grew in prestige. This is doubtless why Saint Michael was among those who spoke to Joan of Arc. "I am Michael, protector of France. Arise and go to the aid of the King of France." And he guided the shepherd girl from Lorraine in her epic bid to crown Charles VII in Reims.

The king, who was trying to reconquer his kingdom, put an able captain, Louis d'Estouteville, in charge of the Mont's garrison. He set about organising the citadel, enabling it to withstand the last English attack in 1434. A fire broke out in the town, destroying the wooden houses and damaging the ramparts. The English tried to take advantage of this by approaching the Mont in large numbers and, with their terrible engines of war, they managed to breach the walls. For a while, they believed the town had fallen but the garrison held out and the English were forced to retreat. The shore was littered with dead bodies. Knights from the Mont retrieved two enormous bombards, setting them up at the entrance to the town, where they can still be seen.

The knights of Saint Michael

At the end of the Middle Ages, the highly devout King Louis XI loved pilgrimages and twice came to visit the sanctuary that symbolised the French victory over the English.

It was this that prompted him to found an order of knighthood with Saint Michael as the first knight. The Duke of Burgundy, who was a great enemy of Louis XI, already had the Knights of the Golden Fleece at his command. The King of France gathered the knights of Saint Michael around him, picked from among the finest noblemen in the kingdom. They wore a collar decorated with golden cockles. Suspended from this was a medal depicting the angel slaying the dragon and engraved with the motto of the order, *Immensi terror oceani* (terror of the immense ocean).

Wearing white damask robes, the dignitaries took part in splendid ceremonies presided over by the king in the Chapel of Saint Michael in the heart of Paris.

Louis XI then had another idea. The ruthless monarch ordered a wood and metal cage to be suspended from the ceiling at the Mont. Every time the prisoner inside moved, the whole contraption began to rock. Being in this confined space in the freezing, lonely old abbey was just like being in hell.

Above

LOUIS XI FOUNDING THE ORDER OF SAINT MICHAEL.

The king sits among the knights of this order of chivalry. Miniature attributed to Jean Fouquet, 15th century, statutes of the Order of Saint Michael.

Paris, BNF (National Library of France), latin ms 19819, fol. 1.

11. - Tombelaine, d'après un dessin trouvé à la Tour de Londres

The islet of Tombelaine

Tombelaine means "little tomb". The islet, just like the Mont, is a granite rock spared from erosion by the sea. It is now deserted but was once a modest replica of the great abbey nearby. It had a chapel and priory. It was also gradually transformed into a citadel. The English captured it during the Hundred Years' War and from there, threatened the garrison on the Mont. In the 17th century, the castle belonged to Fouquet, Finance Minister to Louis XIV. When he fell from grace, the king had the fortifications razed to the ground. Tombelaine, where, according to legend, King Arthur's bride Hélène died, disappeared from History.

The last constructions

Captain d'Estouteville strengthened the abbey's vulnerable defences, encircling it with ramparts and large towers, such as the *Tour du Roi, Tour Cholet, Tour Béatrix* and *Tour de l'Arcade*. With its cannons, machicolations through which projectiles could be dropped, watchtowers and stone sentry boxes overlooking the surrounding area, Mont Saint-Michel was one of the most formidable fortresses of the time.

Louis d'Estouteville appointed his brother Guillaume as Abbot of the

Opposite

THE ISLET OF TOMBELAINE,

the other rock in the bay. It was seized by the English during the Hundred Years' War. At the top of the page, an imagined view of the castle of Tombelaine from a drawing found in the Tower of London.

Town of Avranches.

Mont. His many duties meant that he was unable to devote all his time to the monastery and he left it in the hands of the prior. Thus started the *commendam* system, where the abbot lived outside his community while receiving a substantial part of its revenue. Nevertheless, the cardinal's prestige and political influence facilitated the reconstruction of the church.

Throughout the 16th century, the kings of France visited the famous abbey and François the 1st was received here with great pomp. However, the Wars of Religion threw the kingdom into confusion and the Mont was thrust into a maelstrom of conflict and massacres. Twice, Protestants tried unsuccessfully to take this Catholic stronghold by trickery.

J. P. - 82. - *MONT-SAINT-MICHEL. — Abbaye. - Cachot de Barbès.*
Prisonnier politique en 1842.
The Abbey. - The dungeon of Barbès, a political prisoner.

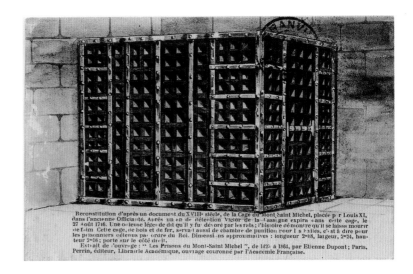

Reconstitution d'après un document du XVIII° siècle, de la Cage du Mont Saint Michel, placée par Louis XI, dans l'ancienne Officialité. Après un an de détention Victor de la Cassigne expira dans cette cage, le 27 Août 1716. Une odieuse légende dit qu'il y fut dévoré par les rats ; l'histoire démontre qu'il se laissa mourir de faim. Cette cage, de bois et de fer, servait aussi de chambre de punition pour les exilés, c'est à dire pour les prisonniers détenus par ordre du Roi. Dimensions approximatives : longueur 2m88, largeur, 2m24, hauteur 2m66; porte sur le côté droit.
Extrait de l'ouvrage : " Les Prisons du Mont-Saint Michel ", de 1425 à 1864, par Etienne Dupont ; Paris, Perrin, éditeur, Librairie Académique, ouvrage couronné par l'Académie Française.

Left

AN OLD PHOTOGRAPH SHOWS THE DUNGEON IN THE MONT WHERE THE POLITICAL PRISONER BARBÈS was incarcerated in 1842.

Right

A RECONSTRUCTION OF THE WOOD AND METAL CAGE ordered by Louis XI. It was used for recalcitrant prisoners.

Archives départementales de la Manche (regional archives).

Prisoners of the Mont

The idea of locking men up to punish them took a long time to catch on. For many years, when sentencing, judges could choose between death, mutilation, public humiliation or a fine. To avoid a public trial or to punish a political opponent, the monarchic government resorted to imprisonment. As nothing had been built specifically for this purpose, they resorted to using citadels such as the Bastille in Paris or fortified monasteries such as the Mont Saint-Michel. When a monastery was used for this purpose, the monastic community was responsible for guarding the prisoners.

The abbey in ruins

Monastic life was on the wane. The monks began to abandon their abbey, some of them preferring to live in the town taverns. The abbots, selected by the king from amongst the finest nobility – such as Abbot de Guise or Cardinal de Montmorency – no longer visited the Mont. An unexpected revival took place when new Benedictines, the Maurists, took it over. These learned men were devoted to the history of the Mont, which they studied from the collection of manuscripts that had built up over the centuries.

The buildings had been badly maintained and were falling into ruin. Three supporting arches in the Romanesque church that had collapsed were not rebuilt but replaced with a very simple classical façade.

Meanwhile, the abbey was converted into a prison, a "Bastille of the sea". The king banished political opponents, debauched aristocrats (often at their families' request) and corrupt priests to the island without trial. The worst, or most recalcitrant, of these were shut up in dark, dank dungeons or in Louis XI's famous cage.

While the Mont had been at the forefront of great innovations in fortifications, Louis XIV and Vauban no longer deemed it essential for the defence of the realm and did little work to it.

Visitors continued to flock to the Mont. The Marquise de Sévigné wrote to her daughter in 1689: "From my chamber I could see the sea and the majestic Mont Saint-Michel, which you beheld in all its pride and that witnessed your beauty…" In 1788, the sons of Philippe, Duke of Orléans, came to visit the Mont Saint-Michel, guided by their governess, a famous novelist and teacher, the Countess of Genlis. The cage, "a barbaric monument" was removed in the presence of the young men. The elder of the two later went on to become King Louis-Philippe I of France in 1830.

THE MONT SAINT-MICHEL SEEN FROM THE PORT OF MOIDREY,
by Paul Huard circa 1840. Before the preservation work was carried out in the 19th century, the
monastery had lost the forbidding appearance it once had during the Middle Ages but this
painting shows that it continued to fascinate artists and travellers alike. Museum of Avranches.

**WHEN IT BECAME POPULAR TO VISIT
HISTORICAL MONUMENTS,**
the town, here pictured circa 1910, welcomed
tourists as it had once welcomed pilgrims.
Henry Decaëns Collection.

The resurrection
of the Mont

The French Revolution scattered the last monks but Mont Saint-Michel remained in use as a prison. The abbey was now nothing more than a gloomy, terrifying gaol. New prisoners were sent here after every riot or failed uprising. Victor Hugo recalled the tragic destiny of these men: "Around us, as far as the eye could see, was infinite space, the blue horizon of the sea, the green horizon of the land, clouds, air, freedom, birds wheeling, ships in full sail; and then, suddenly, above the old walls above our heads, the pale face of a prisoner."

Some of them managed to escape, such as the painter Colombat. He found an old nail during a fire and used it to make a hole in the wall. An accomplice sent him a rope concealed in a loaf of bread. One night, between two patrols, he slipped down the high walls. His escape made him famous overnight. Another prisoner, Barbès, tried to emulate him but, blown by the wind and blinded by fog, he let go of the rope and merely earned himself a bro-

Au Mouton Blanc
ALLIAUME

CAFÉ DE LA POSTE
EPICERIE MERCERIE
BERTRAND

HOTEL
POULARD

Au MOUTON
BLANC
ALLIAUME

BAZAR
DU BON
MARCHÉ

DEJEUNERS & DINERS
SERVIS
SUR TERRASSE
DOMINANT LA MER

5009. - MONT-SAINT-MICHEL

THE RESTORATION OF THE CHURCH.
This early 20th century postcard shows the extent of the work that had to be carried out to save the abbey. Henry Decaëns Collection.

The restoration

Paradoxically, the monastery may have been saved after the French Revolution because it was used as a prison, obliging the state to maintain it when the monastic community disappeared. But the prison authorities adapted the buildings to their needs. Nevertheless, the architectural interest of this monument became increasingly obvious as the Romantic movement rediscovered the Middle Ages. Meanwhile, politicians, administrators and historians were also becoming aware of the need to save endangered historical monuments. This often meant rebuilding from scratch – no easy task as many documents were missing and because the buildings on the Mont had evolved over the centuries. Successive architects combined imagination with reasoning to save and restore the Mont. Edouard Corroyer, Victor Petitgrand and Paul Gout in the 19th century, in particular, were responsible for the Mont's singularly famous outline.

ken leg. The garrison was alerted and he was soon recaptured.

The abbey was rediscovered during the 19th century by Romantic writers and visitors, who admired its extraordinary beauty and architecture. The prison was finally abolished under the Second Empire and in 1874, the Mont became a historic monument. Writers through the years have celebrated this monastery-citadel. In *Ninety-three*, Victor Hugo recalled the "huge, black triangle, crowned with a cathedral and armoured with a fortress" – i.e. the Mont, "which is to the ocean what the Great Pyramid is to the desert…" Théophile Gautier described it rising above the mist "like a huge erratic block, the remains of some antediluvian commotion, in the midst of this flat immensity, uniformly tinted with grey." In *The Sea*, Jules Michelet beheld "a vast, ever-lonely, ash-white plain of shifting sands, whose deceptive smoothness is the most dangerous of traps. It is at once land and sea and no longer land and sea". Guy de Maupassant found it unbelievably strange and beautiful, writing that the abbey was "far away from the land, like a fantastic manor, as bewildering as a palace of dreams". Maurice Barrès described the Mont rising "like a miracle from the quicksands".

The Mont was carefully and painstakingly restored to its former glory, although imagination sometimes won out over accuracy. Current restoration work is much more rigorous, with modern scientific techniques and historical research providing improved understanding of what the Mont used to be like.

The resurrection of a centre of spirituality

After the festivities celebrating the abbey's one thousandth anniversary in 1966, it was taken over by a Benedictine order. In 2001, the Bishop of Coutances and Avranches asked the Jerusalem Monastic Fraternity to take over the abbey. Father Pierre-Marie Delfieux founded this monastic order in Paris in 1975, which, from early on, was associated with a community of nuns. They live near their primary church, Saint-Gervais-Saint-Protais, work part-time in the town and follow the rules of a *Book of life*. Services are marked by ample liturgy in French where chants and music have a privileged place. The Fraternity expanded in France, setting up in Strasbourg, Europe (Brussels and Florence) and worldwide (Montreal). As in Vézelay, the Community now welcomes pilgrims and prays for, and with, visitors to the Mont Saint-Michel.

The abbey has therefore reconnected with its spiritual past and remains a testament to a thousand years' of attempts to serve God, monks and pilgrims alike.

THE COMMUNITY IN PRAYER.
The Mont has returned to its spiritual function, with monks and nuns in residence again.

Ensuring the Mont remains an island

For centuries, polders were constructed around the bay to reclaim land from the sea for grazing sheep. The insular character of the Mont has become compromised. In addition to encroaching farmland, the bay is subject to a natural silting-up and extending salt marshes. The rivers that once streamed over the tidal flats are now tamed and are no longer powerful enough to scour the silt deposited by each tide. Human activity has also played its part in silting-up the bay, with the causeway to the Mont built in 1885, the Roche-Torin dyke to the east and the dam over the Couesnon in 1969 - all inhibiting the free flow of water. When restoring the insular character to the Mont, the surrounding ecosystem must be taken into account. The Mont was listed a World Heritage Site by Unesco in 1979, followed by the bay itself in 1987 – it is an over-wintering spot for migratory birds and a sanctuary for invertebrates, fish and sea mammals. Salt marshes have their own specific vegetation. The bay is also used for

THE FOOTBRIDGE.
This artist's impression shows the footbridge that will replace the causeway and enable sea currents to scour the bay of silt again. (© Syndicat mixte de la Baie du Mont Saint-Michel/Imagence/MG Design)

mussel, oyster and sheep farming. The many projects underway therefore reflect both the growing awareness of this inexorable trend and a desire to restore the natural balance between man and nature. The levelling of the Roche-Torin dyke in the 1980s was the first undertaking. In 1995, after studies were carried out, the various public authorities eventually agreed on a huge restoration project which started in 2006. A new dam over the Couesnon, to be completed in 2008, will serve to retain some of the tidal

FROM THE FOOTBRIDGE.

The picture shows the tide completely surrounding the Mont, which nowadays only happens at particularly high tides. (© Project management team: Feichtinger Architects, Dietmar Feichtinger, architect, Paris/BET Schlaich, Bergermann & Partner, Stuttgart)

waters and release them progressively: thus the silt built up around the rock will be flushed out via a channel on either side. The final thousand metres of the causeway is to be replaced by a footbridge between 2008 and 2011 and, over the last three hundred metres, by a submersible landing area and shuttle service.

THE DAM OVER THE COUESNON RIVER.

This dam will hold back some of the tidal waters, which will then be released progressively to scour out the bay around the rock.

© Luc Weizmann, architect, BRL ingénierie/SPRETEC/ANTEA_Simulation Imagence/MG Design.

Visiting
Mont Saint-Michel

The following section describes the main stages of a tour of the Mont. Once through the town gates, we will discover the town and its ramparts. Then we will make our way to the abbey. This is traditionally where tours start but you can make up your own itinerary.

The town gates

Left page

THE RAILWAY MADE TRAVELLING TO THE MONT EASY.
This poster offered excursions to the Mont from Paris.
Archives départementales de la Manche (regional archives).

THE ENTRANCE TO THE TOWN, protected by three successive gates.

One of the major preoccupations in the Middle Ages was how to fortify the entrance to a town, always a vulnerable spot. Three monumental gates were built here to ward off attacks: the *Porte de l'Avancée*, or forward gate, the *Porte du Boulevard* and the *Porte du Roi*, or king's gate. The third, the king's gate, is protected from the south by two large towers called *Tour de l'Arcade* and *Tour du Roi*. A ditch, a drawbridge and a portcullis made it even more difficult for attackers to enter the town. The coat-of-arms of the abbey, the town and the sovereign, symbols of the three levels of authority, were all carved on the gateway. Guards kept watch from the top of the parapet and were billeted in the *Logis du Roi*, or king's lodgings. Leading up to this gate was the Boulevard and its gate, also designed in the 15th century. One hundred years later, the king's lieutenant completed the defences by building the *Porte de l'Avancée*. This gate is flanked by the townspeople's guardroom (*corps de garde des bourgeois*), who took it in turns to keep watch from here.

The two formidable cannons, taken from the English during the Hundred Years' War and known as *michelettes* or *miquelettes*, show how much military technology had improved, necessitating the strengthening of walls and the entire system of defence.

The town of Mont Saint-Michel and its ramparts

The town

Mont Saint-Michel is also a town, or rather a small Norman village, nestling at the foot of the abbey. The first houses were built on the north side and later, houses were built to the south. Pilgrims would find inns and taverns, just as visitors today find hotels and restaurants. They bought pilgrim badges, just like tourists buy souvenirs. A narrow street leads up to the monastery. The local inhabitants, known as *Montois*, prefer to use a short-cut, Chemin des Monteux. The town has its own church, dedicated to Saint Peter, and a graveyard, watched over by a granite cross standing high above the sea nearby.

The ramparts

During the 15th century, ramparts were built all around the town, interspersed with towers, from the North tower with its lookout post all the way round to the town gates. The technical advances are obvious when these towers are compared to the techniques used during the Middle Ages. The towers were no longer miniature fortresses designed to deal with minor local uprisings. Interconnected by a parapet walk, the towers no longer overlooked the town walls. On the contrary it was the walls that defended the towers in line with the modern principle "whatever provides the defences must itself be defended" (Germain Bazin).

The ramparts run close by the houses in the village. *Tour Boucle* was once known as the bastillion or small bastion. It juts out over the sand and is a forerunner of the achievements of the great military architect Vauban. Horizontal slits were inserted to house bombards, enormous late-Mediaeval cannons. As advances were made in artillery, the defences were improved.

Top
MAISON DES ARTICHAUTS

Opposite
**MÈRE POULARD'S RESTAU-
RANT,** where a famous omelette is prepared.

THE FANILS OR STOREHOUSE,
AND TOUR GABRIEL.

The Fanils or storehouse, and Tour Gabriel (1524)

The Mont's defences were completed by the king's lieutenant Gabriel Dupuy. The tower called after him, *Tour Gabriel*, is a fine example of the advances made in engineering at the time. All possible angles of attack were catered for. The garrison was able to react speedily to any attack, with cannons set deep inside the walls. This large circular bastion, which resembles the bastions in the castle of Fougères, defended the storehouse. A chimney provided an outlet for smoke and, in the 19th century, a windmill was erected on the platform.

The abbey was transformed into a citadel. Although the sheer sides of the rock already afforded ample protection, men throughout the ages tried their best to reinforce the monastery's defences.

Le Châtelet or redoubt was built at the end of the 14th century. In front of it is the barbican, a rectangular forework with crenellated battlements. It is flanked by two handsome turrets, framing either side of the entrance. The staircase that leads up to the guardroom was once closed off by a portcullis. The steps are particularly steep and have been compared to an abyss.

The original entrance to the abbey lay to the north-east before being moved to the east. The gatehouse on the ground floor contains the finest fireplace in the monastery, decorated with luxurious mouldings. At the end of the 14th century, when the Mont became a citadel, it was turned into a guardroom.

Above

ELEGANT LADIES FROM THE BELLE EPOQUE

period giving alms to beggars at the entrance to the abbey.

Henry Decaëns Collection.

Opposite

THE GREAT INNER STAIRCASE

circa 1910, after the steps were restored by Paul Gout.

Henry Decaëns Collection.

The abbey entrance

The great outer staircase, called the *Grand Degré extérieur*, leads from the town to the monastery. During the Middle Ages, grandiose ceremonies were held whenever powerful visitors entered a town or abbey. The abbot received the king at the town gates, the Archbishop of Rouen at the top of the village and the Bishop of Avranches at the entrance to the abbey. Because of this, the architecture formed a majestic backdrop to the slow climb up the rock.

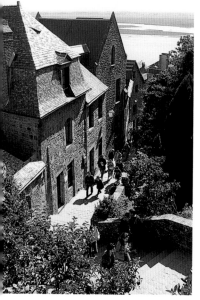

Above

THE MONASTIC TOWN SEEN FROM ABOVE.

Opposite

TO DEFEND THE ENTRANCE TO THE ABBEY, powerful fortifications were required: a forework, the rectangular, crenellated barbican, stands in front of the châtelet, flanked by two turrets.

The great outer staircase runs alongside the abbot's house. Visitors had to use this staircase to access the sanctuary, which ran between two high walls and which was defended from the two fortified bridges connecting the house to the interior of the church. One of the bridges was made of stone with machicolations. It dates from the 15th century and its military function is quite obvious. The other bridge was made of timber and slate and dates from the 16th century.

The great staircase leads to the terrace called *Saut-Gauthier* where the southern doors of the church open out.

The abbey church

The church was built during the 11th century and took about sixty years to complete. It was built on top of the rock which first had to be flattened. This daring construction was fragile and required alteration on several occasions over the years.

The façade of the church and Plomb du four

The buildings fell into disrepair between the 16th and 19th centuries. The plain Romanesque façade, flanked by two towers, disappeared. One of the towers was demolished at the end of the Middle Ages. The other, the clock tower on the south side, survived until the fire in 1776. The first spans of the church, which had collapsed, were replaced by a west-facing platform, called *Plomb du four*. The platform looks out over the Chausey islands to the west. The present sacristy to the left of the façade was originally the monks' dormitory, forming the upper storey of the Romanesque *conventuels*. It stood near the church, providing a shortcut to the monks on their way to Matins.

The church bell tower

Lightning struck the church on numerous occasions, setting fire to the wooden framework. During the Gothic period, a tall spire was erected, flanked by six pyramidal towers. The spire was replaced by an onion-shaped dome in the 17th century and a platform was added in the 18th century to house a semaphore visual telegraph system developed by the Chappes brothers. The architect Petitgrand designed the bell tower that stands here today. Its two Romanesque storeys are crowned with a Gothic spire, a copy of the one in the Cathedral of Notre-Dame in Paris and which is topped by a statue by Frémiet of the Archangel Michael slaying the dragon.

THE ENTRANCE TO THE ROMANESQUE CHURCH.

Left page
THE CHURCH BELL TOWER.
Destroyed and rebuilt several times, its final configuration dates from the 19th century.

Above

THE ABBEY'S COAT OF ARMS.
The shells recall the fact that the abbey once drew pilgrims, who were recognisable from these shells worn on their clothing. The fleur-de-lys, symbolising the French monarchy, proclaimed the King of France as the protector of the monastery.

Above

A ROMANESQUE CAPITAL IN THE CHURCH.

Romanesque art

The concept of Romanesque art only took hold in the 19th century. Until then, everything was classed, somewhat derisively, as "Gothic". As Normandy was a hive of building activity from the 11th century on, these buildings were initially referred to as Norman. Later, to refer to an artistic movement that extended well beyond the confines of Normandy, historians preferred to use the term "Romanesque", in reference to the Romance languages that had evolved from encounters between Latin speakers and the languages of invaders. Richard II, Duke of Normandy appointed Guillaume de Volpiano as Abbot of Fécamp, who reorganised the Norman monasteries, turned the duchy into a breeding ground for bishops and abbots, and encouraged the rebuilding of religious buildings. His ideas significantly influenced Romanesque art throughout Normandy.

The abbey's coat of arms

The abbey's coat of arms, framed with carved drapes, was placed at the entrance to the church in the 18th century. It portrays "a pattern of sable (i.e. black) shells surmounted by a horizontal line of the fleur-de-lys of France". The abbey became a centre of pilgrimage very early on in its existence, as is shown by the cockle shells which marked out pilgrims. The fleur-de-lys, symbolising the French monarchy, proclaimed the King of France as the protector of the monastery. The crosier and mitre, which were sometimes added for decorative purposes, showed that the abbot had the same rank as a bishop.

The Romanesque nave (11th century)

Mediaeval architects brought a sense of movement into the church, breaking up its length with arches and its height with upper storeys. Originally, the nave had seven arches or spans and was completed circa 1084.

At that time, Norman architecture was in its heyday, thanks to the abbot/architect of Fécamp, Guillaume de Volpiano. The Normans used vaulting only in the most sacred parts of their churches. In the nave, they contented themselves with timber rafters, which formed a light barrel vault against the narrow rock.

The original ceiling in the church is thought to have been flat. The timber vaulting is thought to have been built in the 15th century. Abbot Bernard du Bec ordered the construction of the transept crossing with ribbed vaulting, a precursor of things to come. The Romanesque chancel also had a vaulted ceiling but this collapsed in the 15th century.

The north wall of the Romanesque nave (12th century)

The nave in the abbey church shows how much architecture advanced during the Romanesque period. Thereafter, the solidity of the building was based on a framework of pillars and arches rather than on a massive pile of stones. This slenderness, elegance and regularity were not achieved without mishap. One morning in 1103, while the monks were praying, the north wall of the nave collapsed onto the monastery's living quarters. It had to be rebuilt, thicker and with less openwork. Therefore, the southern end of the nave dates from the 11th century while the northern end dates from the 12th century.

In each span, the three storeys are marked out by horizontal banding: the great arcades, the clerestory at the top and the high windows to let in light.

THE ROMANESQUE NAVE.
It had three storeys, great arcades, with the galleries above and above these, the high windows. Long embedded pillars rose to the ceiling of the church, serving as internal buttresses. The wooden framework was used to lessen the weight borne by the walls.

or small columns, all of them similar in appearance. Each colonette forms the base of a rib or arch. There is an ambulatory around the chancel with chapels radiating off it. At the back of the church, the axial chapel was known in the 17th century as Notre-Dame-du-Circuit, the "circuit" being the ambulatory.

The Flamboyant chancel (1450-1521)

The design of the chancel was based on the nave in the abbey church of Saint-Ouen in Rouen, where Guillaume d'Estouteville was also Abbot, and which was considered one of the finest examples of Gothic art. A full four centuries separate the Romanesque nave from the chancel. Everything has been sacrificed to the sense of verticality. The pillars are devoid of capitals and this, combined with

The chancel pillars (mid-15th century).

When the Romanesque chancel collapsed, it had to be rebuilt using new techniques. These ten pillars, completed in the early 16th century, gave the chancel a polygonal layout. Each pillar is shaped like a diamond and consists of a sheaf of colonnettes,

the narrowness of the arches, empha-
sises the impression of verticality.
Each span is also broken up by three
storeys – the arcades, the triforium
and the openwork clerestory, with its
high windows.

The *triforium*, which is supported
by the ambulatory vaulting, skirts the
pillars to avoid weakening them. The
stone tracery lets the light flood in. It
is a masterpiece of Flamboyant Gothic
openwork, with its balustrade supported by trefoiled arches and numerous lancets (elongated pointed
arches), topped by a frieze. The lancets top what F. Enaud termed the
"glass cage" at the top of the chancel.

The chevet (early 16th century)

The unusually high vaulting in the
chancel had a tendency to lean out-
wards and therefore had to be counter-

balanced. Flying buttresses were
used as stone props. Oblique forces
are transferred to enormous vertical
buttresses, made up of two piers that
act as aerial pillars, joined by a wall
topped with tracery. The piers rest
on the dividing walls between the
radiating chapels and are spread out
like a fan. The piers around the chevet are topped by pinnacles, pyramids decorated with stone flowers
and finials that bear witness to the
decorative genius of the period (see
page 18).

The Escalier de Dentelle,
or lace staircase

This finely carved staircase was
built in a pier of the chevet that was
thicker than the others. It leads to a
walkway high above the ground,
connected to the roof of the chancel.

The Romanesque abbey buildings and crypts

In the 11th century, during the Romanesque period, the entrance to the abbey was on the north-west flank of the rock. The buildings were three storeys high, with the dormitory next to the church located above the monks' walkway that itself was supported by the *Salle de l'Aquilon*.

Underpinning the abbey church were crypts, such as the crypt of Notre-Dame-des-Trente-Cierges (Our Lady of the Thirty Candles), which supports the northern arm of the transept. This chapel, where the monks kept the Virgin's clothing, was the spiritual heart of the abbey. The vestibule has a central pillar decorated with Gothic foliage and was once used as a prison (in those days, it was known as the *cachot du diable* or devil's dungeon).

Left page

THE MONT, SEEN FROM THE NORTH-WEST.

In the foreground, the Gothic monastery buildings and *Merveille* are supported by powerful strong buttresses. These stand three storeys high, topped by the refectory on the left and by the cloisters on the right. You can see the space set aside for a further building project that was never accomplished.

Below

NOTRE-DAME DES TRENTE-CIERGES.

Crypts were an additional place of worship in the abbey.

THE MONKS' WALKWAY.
This handsome room, with its ribbed vaulting, was the original abbey during the Romanesque period. Tradition has it that it was used as a walkway by the monks.

Below, **THE CHAPEL OF SAINT STEPHEN.**

The monks' walkway (12th century)

This long chamber beneath the dormitory represents a turning-point in architectural design. Abbot Roger II originally had groined vaulting installed but Bernard du Bec replaced it with ribbed vaulting. This involved using two arches, set between two transverse ribs crossing each other diagonally. This technique, which affords greater fullness to the vaulting, is a forerunner of Gothic art. Two aisles separated by five pillars stand on the rock to the east and the *Salle de l'Aquilon* to the west. Nobody knows what the chamber was originally designed for but tradition has it that it was the Romanesque cloisters, used by the monks for strolling and relaxing, from which it gets its name, *promenoir*.

The building project

You only need walk through the abbey to understand that the monks chose this site to get away from the world and because they wanted to build monuments to honour God and cause wonder among men. Building a large church and abbey buildings on a steep rock was never going to be easy. Underground chapels and crypts support the nave of the church, flanked to the north by a three-storey building and another complex to the west. The *Merveille* was the monks' crowning architectural achievement. Of course, there were accidents along the way; walls and vaults collapsed but the monument survived. However, this architectural achievement was based on a successful dialogue between the community of monks, the anonymous architects – who were probably also monks – and craftsmen. Stones were shipped to the island at high tide from the Chausey islands off the Mont. Stone-masons coaxed granite into the right shape and then, using ropes and wheels or ramps, similar to the one that can still be seen at the Mont, the materials were hoisted up the scaffolding. Once everything was assembled, the wooden scaffolding was removed.

La salle de l'Aquilon (12th century)

The name of an icy wind was given to the Romanesque almonry because it lay on the north face of the rock near the entrance to the Romanesque abbey. The monks welcomed pilgrims in this room with groined vaulting.

Robert de Thorigny's apartments (late 12th century)

Pilgrims followed long vaulted galleries to the south of the abbey. The Romanesque abbot's house stood at the south-western end. It was three storeys high and was the temporal seat of the monastery. On the upper floor, beneath the west-facing platform, were two rooms where the abbot held court. When the Mont was used as a prison, the famous iron cage used to hang from the 11th-century barrel vaulting. Further west, Robert de Thorigny commissioned the building of his austere apartments, which looked out to sea. The gatehouse was on the lower floor, near the entrance. Two dungeons, set into the ground and nicknamed "*in pace*", were used to lock up monks who had fallen foul of the abbot. They became known as the "twins" when the abbey was turned into a prison.

Above

NOTRE-DAME-SOUS-TERRE

Right

THE TREAD WHEEL. This tread wheel resembles the one used by the monks to hoist provisions up to the abbey. The prison authorities are reported to have forced prisoners to walk inside it.

Notre-Dame sous Terre (mid-10th century).

This Pre-Romanesque church dates from the mid-10th century, when the abbey was founded. It has two parallel aisles separated by a wall consisting of two arcades. The Cyclopean wall at the back of the chapel may be a throwback to the former oratory dating from the 8th and 9th centuries. The church, originally freestanding, became a crypt when the Romanesque nave was built above it. It was badly damaged during the 18th century and then restored in the 20th century.

The tread wheel, the ramp (19th century) and the Romanesque ossuary

The Romanesque abbey was extended to the south by buildings designed to accommodate pilgrims. These three-storey tall buildings collapsed in 1817. The only reminder of them nowadays is a detailed scale model which dates from 1701. The infirmary, which has now disappeared, once opened onto the Chapel of Saint Stephen, the mortuary. The monks' ossuary was next to it. The prison authorities later installed a large tread wheel in the ossuary. Prisoners were forced to march inside the wheel to turn it, hoisting provisions up a stone ramp propped against the rock. It was in fact a throwback to the tread wheel formerly used by the monks in the Middle Ages.

The chapel of Saint-Martin

The Crypt of Saint-Martin supports the southern transept of the abbey church. Its semi-circular barrel vault is a model of pure austerity. Stone vaulting was the most important feature of Mediaeval architecture, providing a majestic backdrop for the funeral rites performed at the abbey for noblemen of the day. The vaulting also improved the acoustics for the monks' beloved Gregorian chant.

The crypt known as Gros Piliers (1446-1450)

The Romanesque chancel collapsed in 1421 and war made rebuilding impossible. Once peace was restored, Cardinal d'Estouteville ordered the work to begin. The Crypt des Gros Piliers (mighty pillars) was built in a few short years. It bore the weight of the new chancel, with ten mighty cylindrical pillars, possibly built around the original central Romanesque pillar. Two of these, smaller than the others, were called the palm trees. Prism-shaped ribs bring life to the vaulting, penetrating the pillars and walls at the base. Skilful techniques and a sense of aesthetics of Flamboyant Gothic architecture were used to much success here.

THE CHAPEL OF SAINT-MARTIN.
This austere crypt supports the south transept of the church.

CRYPT KNOWN AS GROS PILIERS

The *Merveille*

The *Merveille* is the Gothic part of the abbey, built after the abbey was destroyed in the early 13th century to replace the Romanesque monastery buildings which were too confined. The eastern wing was built first, on a wide bank and over three storeys, symbolising the social hierarchy during the Middle Ages. The poor were fed on the lower floor, in the almonry, where the groined vaulting is reminiscent of Romanesque traditions. On the second floor, the abbot received the rich and powerful in the *Salle des Hôtes* or Guests' Room. Here the vault is ribbed. Finally, the refectory was for monks, the clergy taking priority over all other social classes in Mediaeval society. A wooden framework was used to avoid weakening the building as a whole. The building was supported by massive external buttresses.

The western section of the *Merveille* was built after the eastern wing and had three storeys. At the top were the cloisters, beneath this was the *Salle des Chevaliers* [Knights' Room] and below that, the cellar. Provisions were hoisted up from the strand below by means of a tread wheel. During the Wars of Religion, a captain tried to enter the citadel in this way. This wing of the abbey was reserved for the monks and formed the backdrop to monastic life. It was intended to build a third complex of buildings even further west, to include the chapter house for the community to hold meetings and assemblies, but the project was abandoned. At the most inaccessible spot, in the north-western corner, was the cartulary, where the monastery archives were kept, proof of its wealth and past heritage. This small airy room stands on top of an enormous corner buttress.

The Gothic *Merveille*, with its high walls, further protected the abbey from attack.

Left page

THE CHURCH CHEVET.
The spire on the bell tower bears a statue of the Archangel by Frémiet.

Opposite

THE BAYS OF THE CLOISTERS
look out over the sea.

THE GOTHIC CLOISTERS.

At the top of the *Merveille*, elegant galleries surround a small garden. This space, between sky and sea, once reserved for monks, was a place for strolling, meditation and conversation.

The cloisters (early 13th century)

The cloisters, located on the top floor of the *Merveille*, was reserved for the monks who used it for strolling, meditation and conversation. Covered galleries surround this roof garden, suspended between sea and sky. The northern transept of the abbey church was shortened to make way for this area. The *lavatorium* or lavabo, with a dou-

ble bench and fountain, were built here at ground level. This was where the abbot would perform a feet washing ceremony, in memory of Christ. The western gallery was intended to open out onto the chapter room but it was never built. What would have been the doorways to the chapter room are now three bay windows.

The colonettes in the cloisters

The shafts are thought to have originally been carved from fine-grained limestone, similar to marble, but this was replaced with fine-grained granite by the architect Corroyer during the restoration work. The hardness of the stone explains the prismatic outline and simplicity of the plinths,

A corner piece in the cloisters

The corner pieces (or squinches) between the arcades of the cloisters are made of soft Caen limestone, ornamented with a wide variety of carvings. Two main designs were chosen: a rose framed with three smaller roses and a leaf pattern that fills the entire triangular section. The cavity carved out in the wall provides a dark background against which the swirling sculptures stand out. Some of the corner pieces are decorated with figures of the Pascal lamb or Christ.

The refectory (early 13th century)

Monastic meals were almost ceremonial occasions and major technical feats were required to embellish the room in which they were taken. As a vaulted ceiling would have been too heavy, the architects preferred to use a semi-circular wooden framework in the form of a huge upturned hull, reminiscent of the Romanesque nave in the church. A thick wall bears the weight of the framework and, in order to avoid weakening it with wide bays, narrow windows, barely wider than slits, were set deep in the walls. Although invisible from the entrance, they fill the room with light. During meals, a monk would read sacred texts from a pulpit in the south wall, his voice filling the whole room thanks to the excellent acoustics. The pantry and kitchen were on the south side of the refectory.

bases and abaci. The colonnettes were laid out in two staggered rows instead of in pairs. They are connected by arcades along the same row and diagonal arches mark out small triangular vaults. This succession of trivets provides great stability to the building.

Top
A CORNER PIECE IN THE CLOISTERS.

Above
THE REFECTORY.

LSalle des Hôtes *or Guests' Room (early 13th century)*

The most important visitors to the abbey took their meals here with the abbot. It contains two aisles where the tables were set out, two huge fireplaces where the meals were prepared and latrines in the north wall – the typical layout of a reception room at the time. The elegance of the ribs and pillars, the light flooding in through the great bay windows and the beauty of the stylised foliage, all testify to Gothic pomp and splendour. Using a style originating in the Paris basin, this room was "one of the most elegant creations of vernacular architecture in the Middle Ages" according to Germain Bazin. To the south, the chapel of Sainte-Madeleine, was where travellers prayed before and after meals.

Salle des Chevaliers *or Knights' Room (early 13th-century)*

This room owes its name to the order of knights of Saint Michael, founded by Louis XI. Yet it seems no meeting was ever held here. It was in fact used as a calefactory, or *chauffoir*, huge fireplaces, their chimney pieces rising to ceiling height, afforded some protection against the cold. Historians believe that tapestries were used to divide the chamber into smaller rooms

Top

THE SALLE DES CHEVALIERS OR KNIGHTS' ROOM (early 13th century). Monks worked in this Gothic-style chamber on the second floor of the Merveille.

Below

THE SALLE DES HÔTES OR GUESTS' CHAMBER. This was where the abbot received noble visitors.

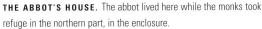

THE ABBOT'S HOUSE. The abbot lived here while the monks took refuge in the northern part, in the enclosure.

BELLE-CHAISE.
Photo: Henry Decaëns.

and to hide the raised passageway to the south so that guests could access the church without disturbing the monks. The room was probably also used as a scriptorium, quite a different place to the calefactory normally found in Benedictine monasteries. It was here that the monks copied and illuminated manuscripts.

The originality of Norman art comes to the fore here: sturdiness wins out over elegance and evolving trends in architectural design are clearly evident here when compared to the earlier *Salle des Hôtes*. The columns are stocky, the ribbed vaulting is accentuated and the almost vertical capitals are decorated with fine carvings of foliage. Large windows let the light flood into the four aisles.

The abbot's house

Abbots lived in close proximity to pilgrims, while the monks remained hidden away in the northern enclosure. The abbot's house, built in stages between the 13th and 16th centuries, runs from east to south beyond the *Châtelet*. The Courtroom, known as *Belle-Chaise*, has narrow windows separated by colonettes and is located above the guardroom. The garrison was billeted in *Tour Perrine*, a large square tower with a pointed roof. This tower is immediately adjacent to the *bailliverie*, where the bailiff, a lay officer, lived. Beyond it were the abbot's house, an impressive building supported by three piers and four relieving arches. Political prisoners were later held here in

what became known as the *Petit Exil* and *Grand Exil*. Finally, the Chapel of Sainte-Catherine-des-Degrés (Saint Catherine of the Steps) and the priory were housed in the last building, near *Saut-Gauthier*. Although vernacular, the architecture had decidedly military strength.

Belle-Chaise

Above the guardroom lay *Belle-Chaise*, the room where the abbot administered justice, for he had the right to sentence anybody on his land. Criminal offences were the sole exception as a man of the church was forbidden to spill blood. The abbot sat on a throne or *chaise* which gave the room its name.

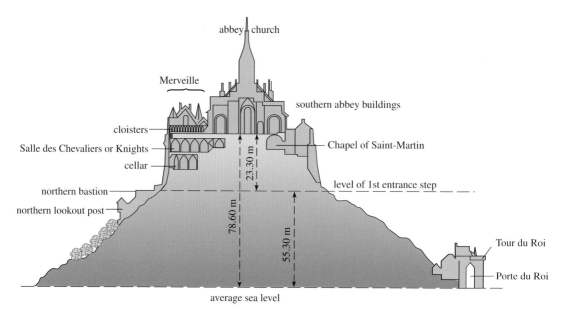

North-south cross section

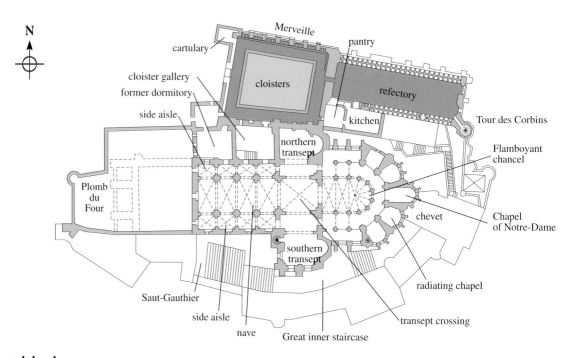

Church level

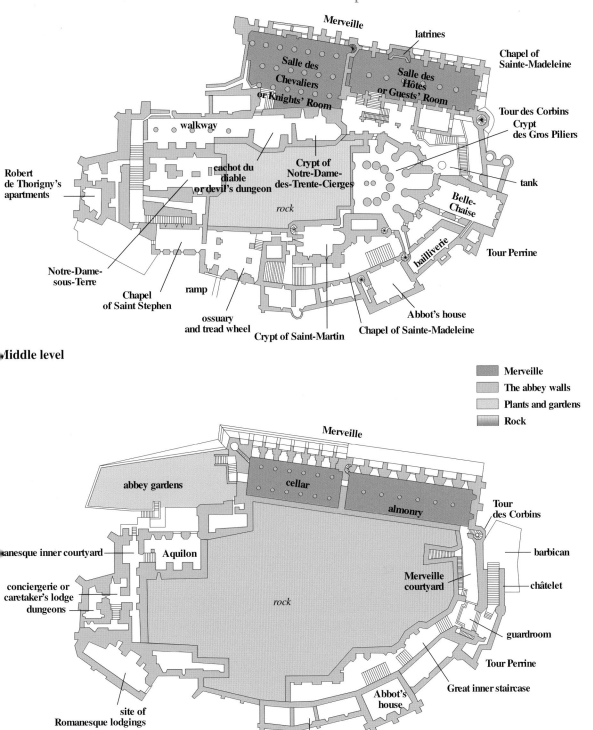

Middle level

Merveille

latrines

Chapel of Sainte-Madeleine

Salle des Chevaliers or Knights' Room

Salle des Hôtes or Guests' Room

walkway

Tour des Corbins

Crypt des Gros Piliers

Robert de Thorigny's apartments

cachot du diable or devil's dungeon

Crypt of Notre-Dame-des-Trente-Cierges

tank

Belle-Chaise

rock

bailliverie

Tour Perrine

Notre-Dame-sous-Terre

Chapel of Saint Stephen

ramp

ossuary and tread wheel

Crypt of Saint-Martin

Chapel of Sainte-Madeleine

Abbot's house

	Merveille
	The abbey walls
	Plants and gardens
	Rock

Merveille

abbey gardens

cellar

almonry

Tour des Corbins

Romanesque inner courtyard

Aquilon

barbican

châtelet

Merveille courtyard

conciergerie or caretaker's lodge dungeons

rock

guardroom

Tour Perrine

Great inner staircase

site of Romanesque lodgings

Abbot's house

Chapel of Sainte-Catherine-des-Degrés

Lower level

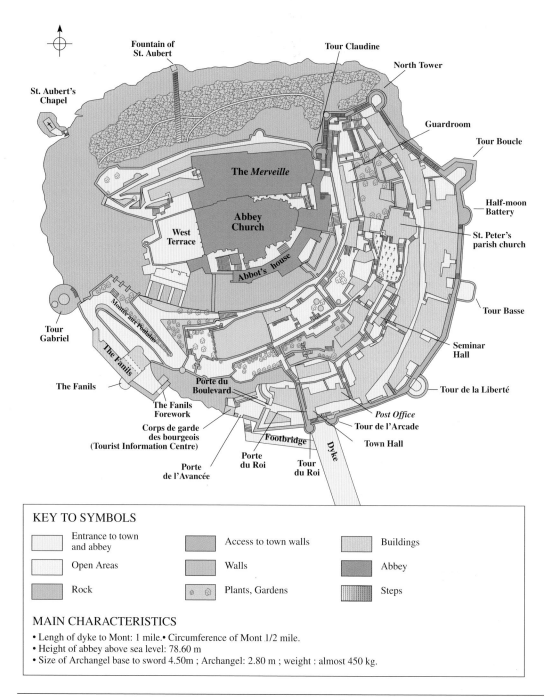

KEY TO SYMBOLS

Entrance to town and abbey	Access to town walls	Buildings
Open Areas	Walls	Abbey
Rock	Plants, Gardens	Steps

MAIN CHARACTERISTICS

- Lengh of dyke to Mont: 1 mile.• Circumference of Mont 1/2 mile.
- Height of abbey above sea level: 78.60 m
- Size of Archangel base to sword 4.50m ; Archangel: 2.80 m ; weight : almost 450 kg.

Editor: Henri Bancaud

Editorial coordination: Solenne Lambert

Graphic design: Studio graphique
des Éditions Ouest-France

Photoengraving: Micro Lynx à Rennes (35)

Printing: Pollina, Luçon (85) - L66921B

© 2008, Éditions Ouest-France, Édilarge SA, Rennes

ISBN 978-2-7373-4476-3

Legal deposit: January 2008

Publisher no: 5659.07.1,5.01.14

Printed in France

Visit us at www.editionsouestfrance.fr